Costume and Ornament of the Middle Ages
In Full Color

Henry Shaw

Edited by
CAROL BELANGER GRAFTON

DOVER PUBLICATIONS, INC.
Mineola, New York

Bibliographical Note

This Dover edition, first published in 2006, is a new selection and layout of illustrations compiled from *Dresses and Decorations of the Middle Ages* by Henry Shaw, originally published by William Pickering, London, in 1843; and from Shaw's *Decorative Arts of the Middle Ages*, originally published by William Pickering, London, in 1851.

DOVER *Pictorial Archive* SERIES

Library of Congress Cataloging-in-Publication Data

Costume and ornament of the Middle Ages in full color / Henry Shaw.
        p. cm. — (Dover pictorial archive series)
    Illustrations compiled from: Dresses and decorations of the Middle Ages / by Henry Shaw. London: W. Pickering, 1843; and The decorative arts of the Middle Ages, ecclesiastical and civil / by Henry Shaw. London: W. Pickering, 1851.
    ISBN 0-486-44765-0 (pbk.)
    1. Decoration and ornament, Medieval. 2. Costume—History—Medieval, 500–1500. 3. Shaw, Henry, 1800–1873. Dresses and decorations of the Middle Ages—Illustrations. 4. Shaw, Henry, 1800–1873. Decorative arts of the Middle Ages—Illustrations. I. Grafton, Carol Belanger. II. Series.

NK1260. C67 2006
745.4094'0902—dc22   2005056070

Manufactured in the United States of America
Dover Publications, Inc., 31 East 2nd Street, Mineola, N.Y. 11501

NOTE

Between 1840 and 1880, Victorian tastes leaned ever increasingly toward an artistic interest in the Middle Ages. A leading proponent of the gothic revival in the decorative arts, Henry Shaw (1800–1873) drew inspiration from this exceptionally rich time in art history. An antiquarian scholar and watercolorist, Shaw produced several books on manuscript illumination as well as on medieval and Elizabethan art and architecture. His fascination with initial letters and other medieval-style dress and ornamentation culminated in the publication of *Dresses and Decoration of the Middle Ages* (1843) and *The Decorative Arts of the Middle Ages* (1851).

Culled from the best of Henry Shaw's volumes, the present edition reproduces, in full color, a selection of costumes and motifs from the dawning of the Middle Ages up to the seventeenth century. Although the lavish apparel of royalty and nobility clearly dominate Shaw's work, costumes of ecclesiastics, crusading knights, and commoners are also represented. In addition, the images within this book offer a chronicle of nearly all aspects of medieval life, from scenes of tournaments with knights in combat, to a portrait of English poet Geoffrey Chaucer, to authors presenting their illuminated books to generous patrons. During this golden age of book creation, a richly illuminated volume was considered a highly prized gift bestowed exclusively upon princes and nobles. Also depicted here are resplendent images of such fine accessories as headdresses, jewelry, and a coronation spoon, a utensil used to hold the oil that anointed the monarch at a coronation ceremony. Ornate candlesticks, sacred reliquaries, elaborately embellished letters, and stunning embroidery designs detail just a small portion of the other decorative ornaments that comprise this volume.

The illustrations selected from Shaw's books draw upon a wealth of authentic primary sources, including illuminated manuscripts, intricately woven tapestries, stained glass church windows, and more. Showcasing the various changes in costume and ornamentation throughout the Middle Ages, this compendium of colorful fashions and decorative motifs may be used as a valuable sourcebook for designers and cultural historians. Where possible, captions identify the illustrations.

Courtiers of the Time of Richard II

John Talbot, Earl of Shrewsbury, Presenting His Book to Queen Margaret, 1445

Princess Elizabeth, 1545

Queen Margaret of Scotland, 1483

Gilbert de Clare, Earl of Clare

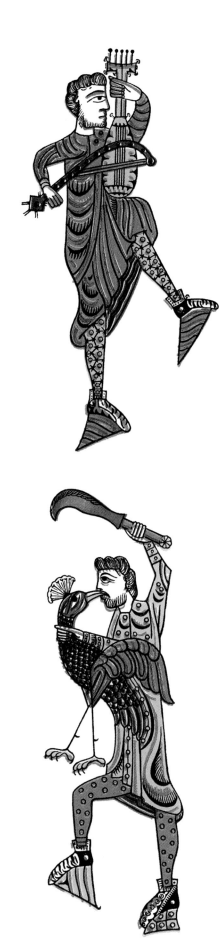

Stained Glass at Bourges Cathedral,
13th century

Occleve Presenting His Book to Henry V, 1410

The Lady Anne, wife of Richard III

A Knight of the Garter, 1470

6

Margaret, Queen of Henry VI and Her Court, 15th century

King John, 1440

The Mitre of Thomas à Becket

9

Stained Glass at Chartres Cathedral, 13th century

Heralds Announcing the Death of Charles VI to His Son, 1500

Queen Phillippa, 1525

Arthur, Prince of Wales, 1502

Birth of St. Edmund, 1433

Figures from tapestries, 16th century

13

St. Catherine, from a painted enamel, 15th century

A Hanap, with cover

14

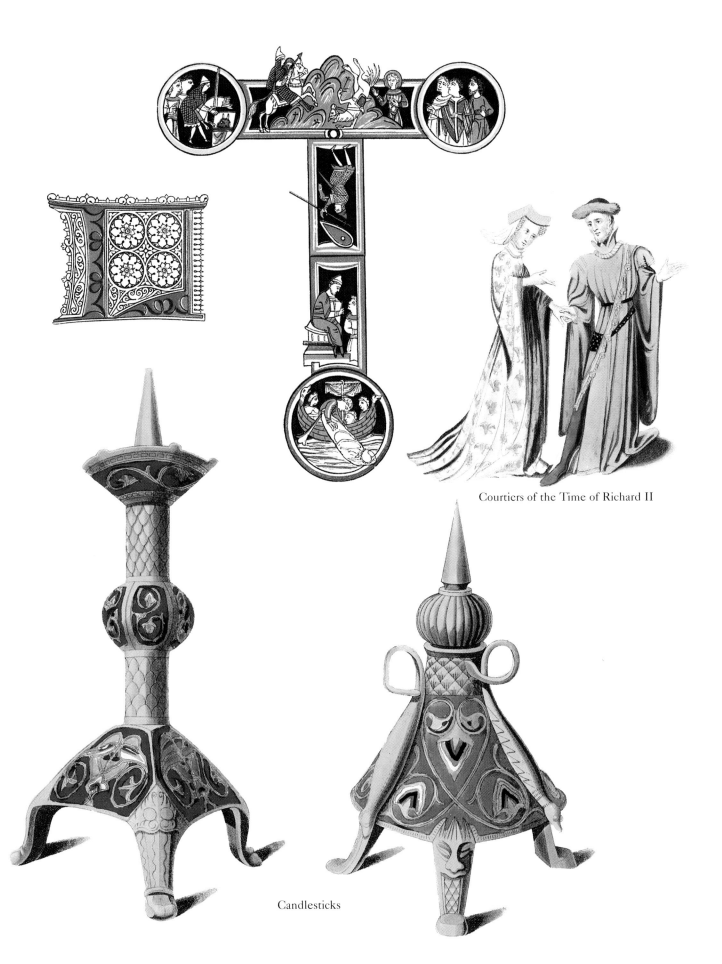

Courtiers of the Time of Richard II

Candlesticks

Pyrrhus Receiving the Honor of Knighthood, 15th century

An Enameled Pendant,
16th century

(reverse)

A Spanish Necklace

Cup in the Queen's Collection,
Windsor Castle, 1540

Saint Agnes by Lucas Van Leyden, 1520

Queen Leanora of Arragon

Queen Johanna of Castile

The Sovereigns of Europe Worshiping St. George, 15th century

Knights Fighting

A Triptych of Encrusted Enamel, Belonging to the Earl of Shrewsbury, 12th century

A Figure of a Saint in Encrusted Enamel, 11th century

An Hourglass, mid-17th century

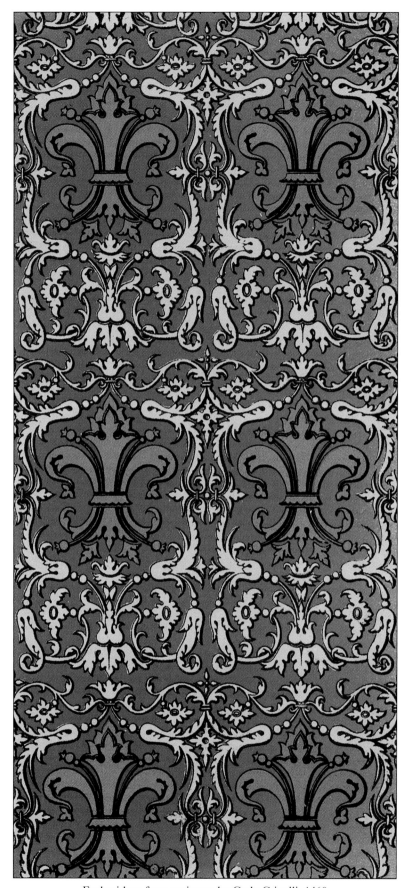

Embroidery from a picture by Carlo Crivelli, 1460

Cup Belonging to the Company of
Goldsmiths, 1558

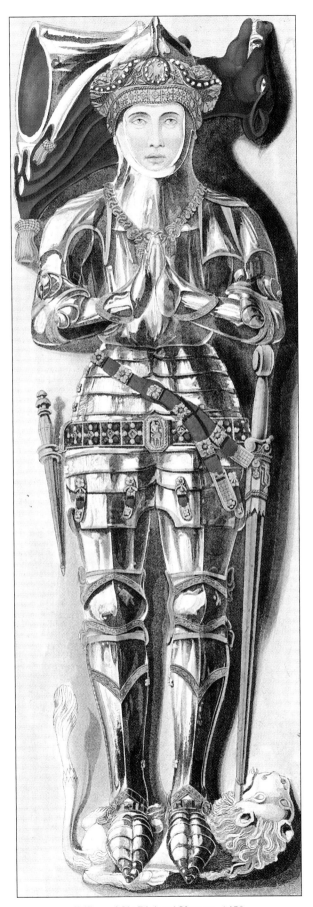

Effigy of Sir Richard Vernon, 1450

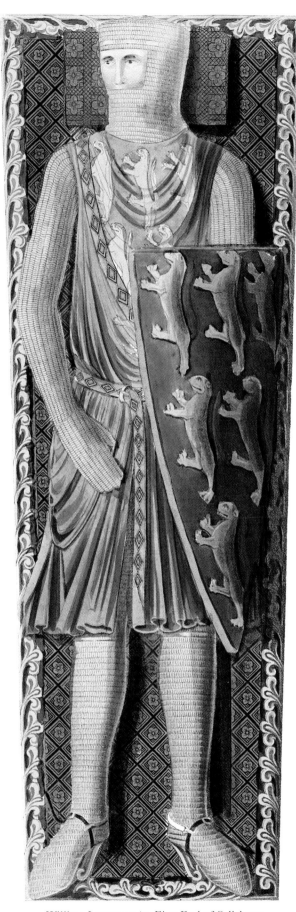

William Longuespée, First Earl of Salisbury

23

Edward III, 1355

The Coronation Spoon

The Coronation Spoon
(reverse)

The Black Prince, 1355

25

Philip, Duke of Burgundy, 1460

King Henry I, 1440

Stained Glass at Bourges Cathedral, 13th century

King John of Portugal

From *The Romance of the Rose*, 1480

Ladies Playing on the Harp and Organ

Poverty, from *The Romance of the Rose*, 1480

Old age, from *The Romance of the Rose*, 1480

Masque of Charles VI of France, late 15th century

King, late 12th century

Pastoral Staff of the Abbey of Lys

Henry VI and His Court, 15th century

Burial of Edward the Confessor, 13th century

Proclamation of a Tournament, 1450

From *The Romance of
the Rose*, 1480

The Clasp of the Emperor Charles V, 1530

Ornamental portions
of a dagger, designed
by Holbein, early
16th century

A Pulpit Hanging, 16th century

Stained Glass at Soiffons Cathedral, 13th century

Incised slab, 1350

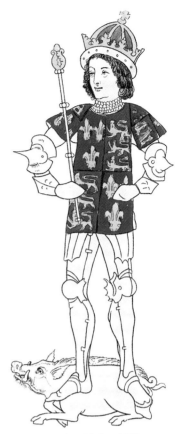

King Richard III

Richard Nevil, Earl of Salisbury

Coat of Arms

Minstrels, 1480

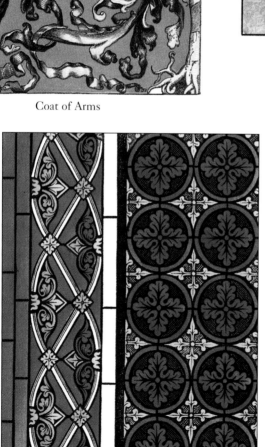

Stained Glass at Bourges Cathedral, 13th century

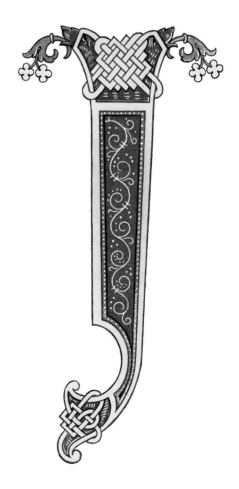

Pope Sixtus IV, ca. 1471–1484

Constancia, Duchess of Lancaster, wife of John of Gaunt, 1525

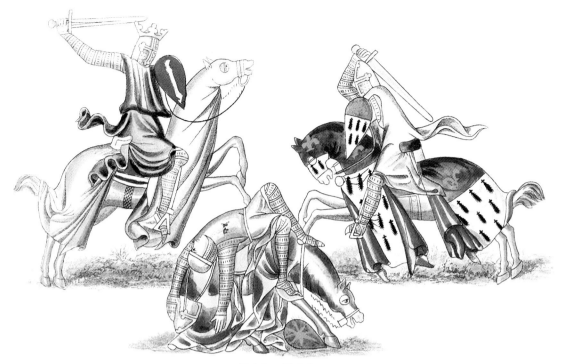

Knights Fighting

Christine de Pisan, Presenting Her Book to the Queen of France, 15th century

The Limerick Mitre, 1408

Part of a room, from a picture by John Schoreel, 1520

Shooting at the Butt, 1496

Stained Glass at Bourges Cathedral, 13th century

Ornamental portions of a sword,
designed by Holbein,
early 16th century

Tobit, 1470

Book Cover, 16th century

From *The Romance of the Rose*, 1480

Elevation of the Host, 1500

From *The Romance of the Rose*, 1480

Horse and Attendant, 1511

45

Headdresses

Purse, 16th century

Richard II, 1377

46

Stained Glass from the Church of St. Peter, Hereford, 14th century

47

Niello Cup, late 15th century

Ornament on Chasuble

Margaret, Queen of James III of Scotland, 1483

A Silver Reliquary

49

Stained Glass at Bourges Cathedral, 13th century

King Alfred's Jewel

Cross from Mount Athos

Ring of King Athelwulf

Geoffrey Chaucer

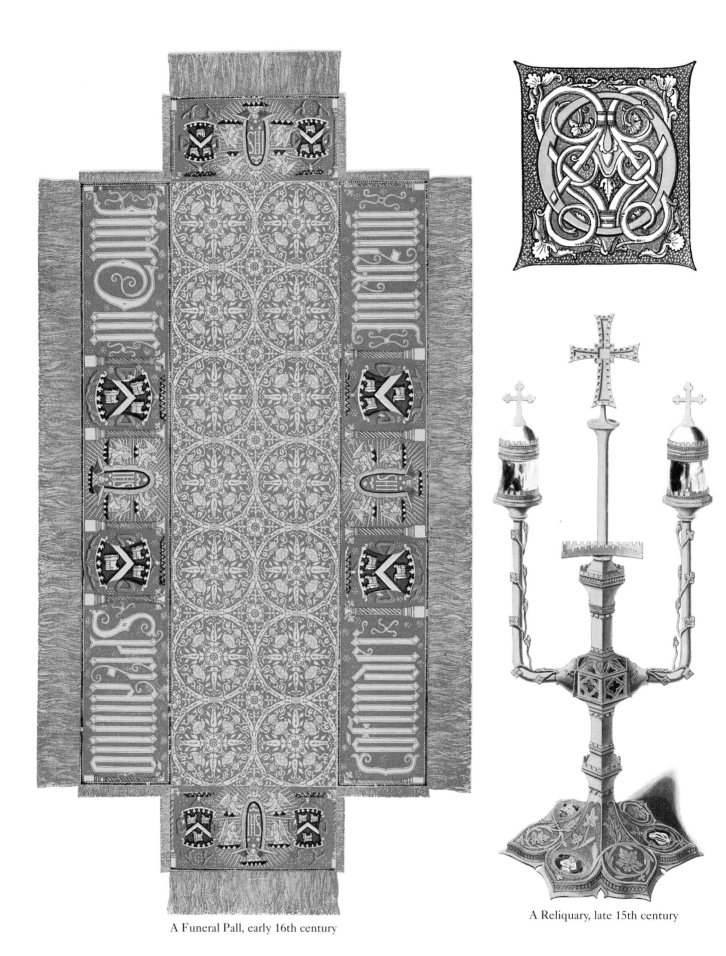

A Funeral Pall, early 16th century

A Reliquary, late 15th century

Troy Town, between 1498–1515

A Pyx, from a Drawing by Vertue, 12th century

A Morse, early 14th century

Henry Beauchamp, Duke of Warwick

God spede ye plouz·ₐ sende us korne ₐ nolk

A Chalice, 1290

A Pair of Bellows (reverse), 1587

Richard de Beauchamp, Earl of Warwick

The Canterbury Pilgrimage, late 15th century

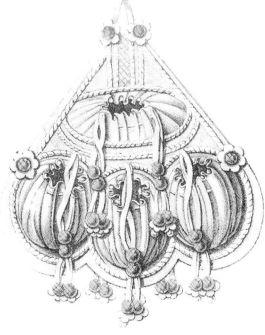

Purse, 16th century

Knight, late 12th century

A Pyx in the Form of a Dove, 12th century

The Lady of the Tournament Delivering the Prize, 1450

Spanish Warriors

Processional Cross, 1360

Francis the First, King of France

The Earl of Surrey, 1540

Ecclesiastics of the 12th century

Stained Glass

Headdresses

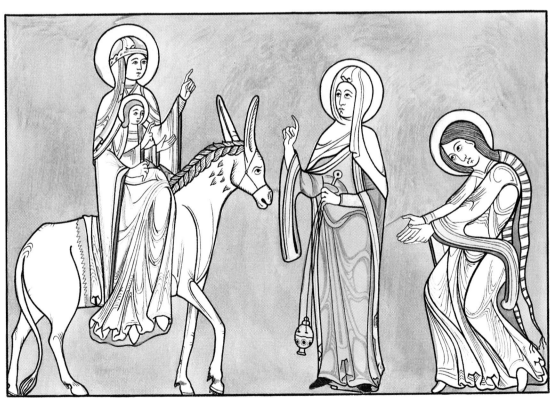

Female Costumes, 12th century

Headdresses

Isabella, wife of William Beauchamp

From a brass in the Church of St. Mary Key Ipswich, 1525

73